D0600776

Grandma's Gumbo

Grandma's Gumbo

Written and Illustrated by
Deborah Ousley Kadair

PELICAN PUBLISHING COMPANY
Gretna 2003

With love and admiration to my grandmothers,
Hettie Gill and Nora Ousley (and a special thanks to
Penny Stockwell—Mimzie—your gumbo is truly yumbo!)

The word "Pelican" and the depiction of a pelican are trademarks
of Pelican Publishing Company, Inc., and are registered
in the U.S. Patent and Trademark Office.

Library of Congress Cataloging-in-Publication Data

Kadair, Deborah Ousley.
    Grandma's gumbo / written and illustrated by Deborah Ousley Kadair.
        p. cm.
Summary: Rhyming text describes the ingredients that go into Grandma's
gumbo. Includes a recipe for Louisiana gumbo.
    ISBN 1-58980-133-4 (hard cover : alk. paper)
    [I. Gumbo (Soup)—Fiction. 2. Grandmothers—Fiction. 3. Stories in
rhyme.] I. Title.
    PZ8.3.K103 Gr 2003
    [E]—dc21
                            2002156417

Printed in Korea
Published by Pelican Publishing Company, Inc.
1000 Burmaster Street, Gretna, Louisiana 70053

Grandma's Gumbo

Something cold, something hot—
Put it in my big black pot.

In my pot that's oh so jumbo,
Just the size for Grandma's gumbo.

Now it's time to make the roux.
That's the first thing we must do.

A little oil, some flour too—
Let it simmer; now it's through.

Two cups of rice will be just fine.
We'll set it aside until we dine.

Don't forget the pinch of salt.
The boiling we don't want to halt.

Sauté some celery until it's tender.
An excellent flavor it's sure to render.

Add an onion; don't shed a tear.
It's just the next ingredient, dear.

Just the thing to make it yumbo,
All a part of Grandma's gumbo.

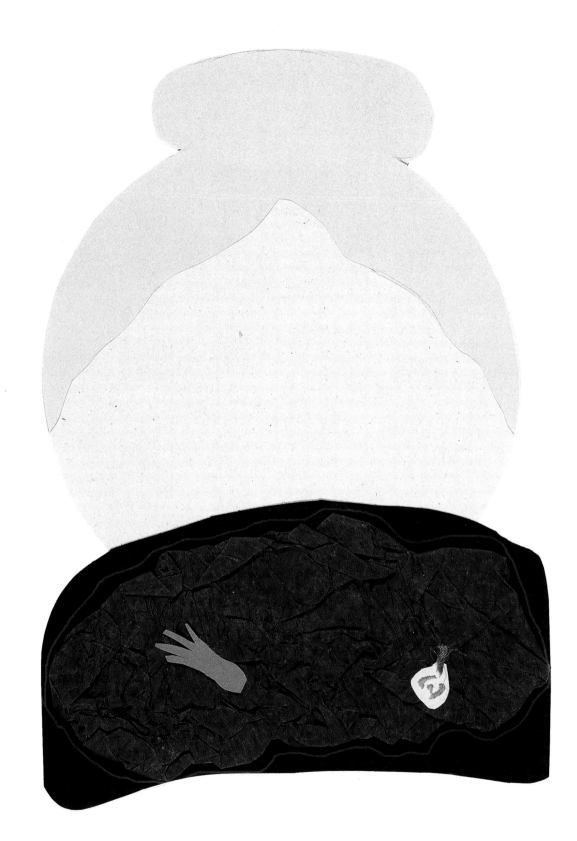

A green bell pepper for the reason
Of bringing out the perfect season.

Okra and tomatoes will be just great.
The flavor we want to regulate.

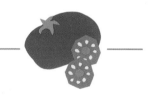

Just the thing to make it yumbo,
All a part of Grandma's gumbo.

Jumbo shrimp, the seafood creature—
Add some to this Creole feature.

In go oysters by the bunch.
They'll give the dish an extra punch.

Just the thing to make it yumbo,
All a part of Grandma's gumbo.

The crab into the pot must go.
Make it fast so he won't know.

Then come green onions, chopped just right.
Add some garlic, a cook's delight.

Just the thing to make it yumbo,
All a part of Grandma's gumbo.

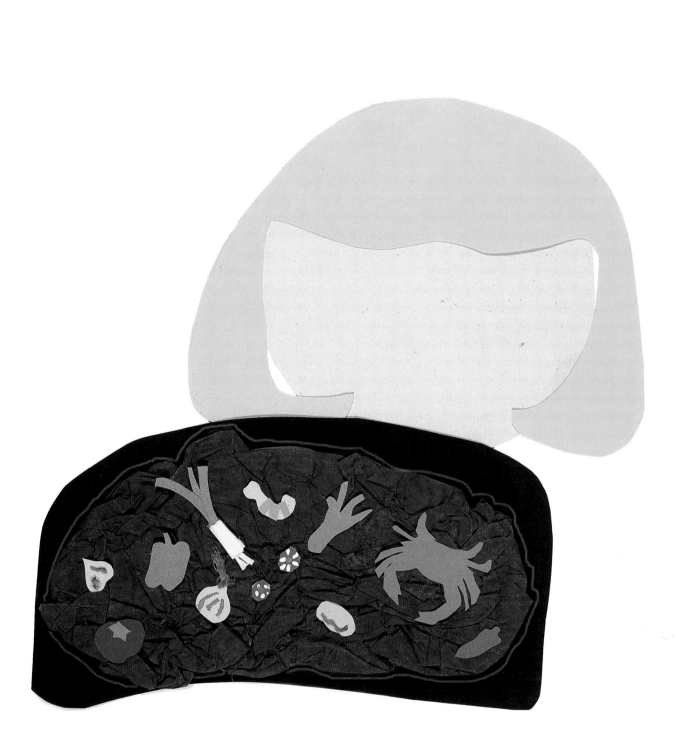

Toss some parsley in the mix,
To help make sure the flavor kicks.

Shake in some hot sauce; don't be shy.
It'll be so good, you'll want to cry.

Come and get it while it's hot.
Scoop it right out of the pot.

Top it off with a dash of filé.
"Oooh ya-ya" is what we'll all say.

Just the thing to make it yumbo,
All a part of Grandma's gumbo.

Grandma's Gumbo

Canola oil
Flour
1 cup chopped celery
2 cups chopped onions
½ cup chopped green bell pepper
1 gal. warm water
1 10-oz. pkg. frozen sliced okra
1 15-oz. can stewed tomatoes with juice
2 lb. fresh peeled, deveined shrimp
1 pt. fresh oysters with juice
1 pt. crab claws
Green onion tops
4-6 garlic cloves, chopped
½ cup fresh chopped parsley
Hot sauce to taste, if desired
Dash of filé powder

Cover bottom of gumbo pot with oil. Pour in enough flour to absorb oil. Brown well, stirring constantly (do not burn).

When the roux is brown, add celery, onions, and bell pepper. Sauté until soft. Add water, okra, and tomatoes with juice.

In a separate pan, sauté shrimp until pink. When okra is tender, add shrimp. Cook for 20 minutes.

Add oysters with juice and crab claws. Cook for 10 minutes. Add green onion tops, garlic, parsley, and hot sauce. Add filé to thicken gumbo. Cook for 5 more minutes. Serve over cooked rice.